UP TO THE MOUNTAIN

Learning His Ways on the Colorado Fourteeners

Jesus is the Only Way!
Di Mathis :)

DIANE MATHIS

DEDICATION

To my Lord Jesus, thank You for being a personal God and using something I love to speak into my heart. I truly desire to follow You all the days of my life. I love You.

To my husband, Scott, thank you for loving me so well and for allowing me to have this journey with the Lord. It took faith and sacrifice on your part, but you let me go. I love you.

To my children and my children's children, this book was written for you. Jesus is the only Way. I love you.

CONTENTS

PREFACE

I grew up in the mountains of Colorado, and always loved hiking in the Rockies, but it wasn't until the spring of 2007, that I heard about the Colorado fourteeners (the fifty-four mountain peaks above fourteen thousand feet). By this time in my life, I'd been married twenty-two years, had raised two incredible kids, and was living in Nebraska facing the empty nest stage that every mom encounters. My husband and I were at a Pastor's Retreat in Colorado called Sonscape, when someone started talking about the Colorado fourteeners and the hiking trails that led to the top of each one. It was at that moment, I caught the *fourteener fever!* When I got home, I started researching the mountains and with the encouragement of my husband, I set a new goal in my life and called it: *fifty-four at forty-four!* (I wanted to summit all fifty-four Colorado fourteeners, starting at the age of forty-four). Before it was over, fifty-four had increased to fifty-eight because of four unofficial fourteeners I wasn't aware of, that I added to my list.

But it was never just about the physical challenge. I also wanted the hikes to be a time of spiritual renewal and challenge. I wanted the Lord to teach me on the mountain. Needless to say, I was pretty excited when I came across Micah 4:2 in my Bible one week before I hiked my first fourteener: "Come, let us go up to the mountain of the Lord... He will teach us His ways so that we may walk in His paths." This became my theme verse as I hiked, and the Lord was faithful to teach me His ways by taking something from each hike and comparing it to the Christian hike of life I was on. Little did I know what adventures and lessons were before me!

By God's grace, I completed my goal in seven summers. When it was all said and done, I had hiked with over sixty different people, led three hiking retreats with women from my church, hiked in all kinds of weather, wore out three pair of hiking shoes, experienced a few close calls, and fell in love with my Maker all over again!

So grab your trekking poles and join me as I take you up to the mountain and share what the Lord taught me on these amazing adventures! I pray the lessons will be as encouraging to your heart as they were to mine.

Diane Mathis

SUMMER 1:
2007

1

Pikes - Misconceptions

Date: Friday, June 29, 2007   **Elevation**: 14,110 feet
Trail Length: 13 miles   **Time**: 5:30am–12:00pm(6 ½ hours)

I had some misconceptions about fourteeners before I started hiking them. The biggest one was I thought it was going to be easier than it was. Don't get me wrong, I knew it would be hard, but I've been athletic all my life. I was a collegiate athlete, so I've experienced pushing my body past what I thought it could do. I've had two babies, and what's more painful than that, right? But that was many years ago, and I think my body had long forgotten that kind of pushing!

The first fourteener I chose to hike was Pikes Peak - thirteen miles to the top. (Why did I choose one of the longest hikes to start with? You tell me!) On the morning of the hike, I was on the trail and hiking by five o'clock, and by five-thirty, I literally thought I was going to die! I had been training for months, but there I was, sucking air like none other. My heart was pounding so hard I thought, "Diane, what in the world have you gotten yourself into this time? You can't even make it thirty minutes. You've only gone one mile. You still have twelve to go…you and your crazy goals!" But I took a few deep breaths (and some of that wonder drug called Advil), and on I hiked. Once my body acclimated I was better, but it was definitely harder than I ever imagined, and one of the most physically demanding days of my life. When I got to the summit and took a look around though, I was hooked. Misconceptions and all, I loved it! One down - only fifty-seven more to go!

I find the same holds true in the Christian hike of life, in that there are many misconceptions about this hike, as well. And I think there are misconceptions because we believe other sources, instead of the source itself (the Bible). We believe what the television, movies, and other people say about God instead of reading God's Word to see what He says.

One major misconception about the Christian hike of life is that there are many trails to God, many ways to get to heaven. But Jesus said, "I am the way the truth and the life. No one comes to the Father except through me." (John 14:6) The Bible teaches there is only one way to heaven - Jesus is the Way. The Christian hike starts only when you believe and trust in Jesus as your Savior.

But I personally had another misconception about the Christian hike. Just like I thought hiking fourteeners would be easier, I thought the Christian hike would be easier too! And when I got further up 'the Christian trail' and realized it wasn't, I thought *"What's the difference?"* It took me time to learn that Jesus never promised to make my life easier as a Christian or fix all my problems here on earth. What He did promise was: if I took His trail, He would lead me to the ultimate and eternal summit of heaven. He would give me the strength to get there, and He would hike with me every step of the way! And that's a *big difference*! I was no longer hiking solo; I was no longer hiking in my own strength, and I was no longer hiking lost!

Side note: Pikes Peak is one of two fourteeners where you can drive to the top. It also has a train that takes you up and down, so I had made arrangements to catch the train instead of hiking down. I got on the train with several foreigners who were touring the mountain. I know I looked as exhausted as I felt, and I'm sure I didn't smell much better. Within minutes, I was asleep, but halfway down the mountain, I woke up with the foreigners all staring at me. It was kind of embarrassing when I realized I'd been drooling extensively. Don't foreigners drool?

On the summit of Pikes Peak

2

Elbert - Downhill Dangers

Date: Wednesday, July 11, 2007   **Elevation**: 14,433 feet
Trail Length: 9 miles RT   **Time**: 7:30am–1:00pm (5 ½ hours)

Mount Elbert was next on my fourteener list and my son, Shane, hiked it with me for my birthday! Elbert is the highest peak in Colorado. Unlike Pikes Peak, which had a lot of switchbacks, Elbert's trail went straight up a slope that looked gentle until you got on it. It was steep! The annoying thing about this trail was its false summits, but we just kept hiking and made it to the real summit in three and a half hours. Words can't describe the beauty I see on a fourteener with mountains in every direction. There were twenty people on the summit, and I wondered if they were worshipping the creation or the Creator.

Since I didn't hike down Pikes, this was my first fourteener descent, and I honestly had the mind-set that all I had to do was make it to the top because going down would be easy - wrong again! Nothing is easy on these massive mountains. There were several times I tripped and almost face planted because I wasn't paying attention.

Spiritually speaking, I was reminded of a Christian's descent from a spiritual mountain-top experience with the Lord. Whether it's a retreat, a spiritual break-through, a mission's trip, etc., we tend to have the mind-set that coming down off the spiritual mountain is going to be easy, and everything is going to be great. But just as I had to be very attentive and focused coming down the fourteener, Christians need be very attentive and focused on Christ when coming off a spiritual mountain-top. Otherwise, Satan or the Christians' own sinful nature will surely trip them up. I've seen many Christians (including myself) who quickly hit a spiritual low after being on the mountain-top with God. I know for me, it was because I wasn't attentive on Christ coming down. I thought I could coast on my own for a while. The reality is though; I need Christ continually every moment of every day whether I'm on an uphill or downhill slope of life!

*The Sovereign Lord is my strength! He will make me as surefooted
as a deer, able to tread upon the heights.
(Habakkuk 3:19, NLT)*

*The Lord directs the steps of the godly.
He delights in every detail of their lives. Though they stumble,
they will never fall, for the Lord holds them by the hand.
(Psalm 37:23-24, NLT)*

Elbert — the highest peak in Colorado

3 - 4
Grays and Torreys - Cairns of Life

Date: Saturday, July 21, 2007   **Elevation**: 14,270 feet / 14,267 feet
Trail Length: 9 miles RT   **Time**: 6am–12pm (6 hours)

My somewhat-reluctant daughter, Courtney, hiked these two fourteeners with me. I guess she didn't want to be outdone by her little brother! We made an overnighter of it and had a great time together. Since I live in western Nebraska, it takes six hours of driving just to get to most of the mountain ranges in Colorado, so I have to travel the day before each hike. This trailhead was a few miles from Georgetown and the four-wheel drive road leading up to it had huge rocks and dips and seemed to go straight up the mountain. It was my first experience at four-wheel driving, so it took us thirty minutes to go four miles! We got to the trailhead parking lot around eight that night and pitched our tent (which was the back end of my son's Bravada)! Courtney slept pretty well, but I was up all night watching the seemingly endless flow of vehicles pulling into the parking area. I'm amazed by how many people hike these fourteeners!

We hit the trail at six o'clock, and like the other trails, it was pretty steep for the first thirty minutes. Courtney told me later in the hike she had serious doubts she could make it, but she hung in there, and once her body acclimated she did great! We enjoyed the beautiful wild flowers and mountain streams. We made it to the summit of Grays at nine o'clock, and it was pretty chilly on top. We quickly ate our PBJs and took off for Torreys. Unlike the trail on Grays that had several switchbacks, the trail on Torreys went straight up a very steep ridgeline. We summited it at ten o'clock with jelly legs but joyful hearts!

I started to notice the piles of rocks beside the trails on these fourteeners. The mountain books call them cairns, but they look like rock altars to me. They're all shapes and sizes, but their purpose is to give direction to the hikers! There were so many rock altars (cairns) on this trail that Courtney and I started to say, "It's time for an altar call" whenever we needed a break (which was quite often)!

I did a word study on altars in the Bible when I got home, and I liked what I found. From the very beginning of time, God instructed His people to build altars. An altar was not only a place of worship where sacrifices were offered, but also a place that symbolized notable encounters with Him.

At one of our altar calls on the mountain, Courtney and I talked about the Mathis family altar we have in the DeBeque Canyon of Colorado. It is the place where God intervened in my husband Scott's life, saved him, and as a result, completely changed the direction our family was heading. We named the rock Ebenezer Rock, meaning "thus far has the Lord helped us." (1 Samuel 7:12) As the kids were growing up, we visited our Ebenezer Rock on occasion, celebrating communion together as a family and thanking God for giving us a new life and a new direction!

Courtney and me on the summit of Grays Peak

5 - 6

Evans and Quandary - In the Clouds

Date: August 3-4, 2007   **Elevation**: 14,264 feet /14,265 feet
Trail Length: 2 ½ miles RT / 7 miles RT
Time: 11:00am-1:00pm (2 hours) / 6:00am-11:00am (5 hours)

Since I had seen so many dogs on the fourteeners, I decided to take my miniature schnauzer, Duke, as my hiking buddy on this trip to see if he'd like it. I left home at six in the morning and arrived at the Evans trailhead (near Idaho Springs) five hours later. I decided to start Duke with a shorter hike to see how he'd do, and I must say, I thought he did all right for a little fella. Every once in a while he would just sit down and not budge and look at me as if to say, "Are you serious?" Then, after a lengthy break, he'd start going again.

When we summited at noon, there were a lot of people on the summit because (like Pikes Peak), you can drive to the top of Evans. There were also several mountain goats, so needless to say, the summit was very crowded! Duke seemed to enjoy the descent much better, so after getting back to the car, I decided to drive to the trailhead of Quandary Peak (near Breckenridge) and car camp. It rained on and off all evening, but by morning it was another beautiful day in the Rockies. Duke and I hit the trail at six o'clock, and it smelled so good walking through the pine trees. When we got above tree line, I could see a big white cloud sitting on top of Quandary. As I hiked into the cloud, I thought about how the Lord came down in a cloud over Mt. Sinai and passed over Moses.

Then the LORD came down in a cloud and stood there with him, and he called out his own name, Yahweh. The LORD passed in front of Moses, calling out, "Yahweh! The LORD! The God of compassion and mercy! I am slow to anger and filled with unfailing love and faithfulness. I lavish unfailing love to a thousand generations. I forgive iniquity, rebellion, and sin. But I do not excuse the guilty."
(Exodus 34:5-7a, NLT)

By the time I summited, the cloud had moved on, but God's presence remained. I know the Lord is always with me, but for some reason, I especially sense His presence when I hike these fourteeners. Thank You Lord, for the compassion, mercy, love, faithfulness, forgiveness, and justice You've show in my life. Yahweh! I worship You!

Side note: Duke will not be hiking with me again. He was not impressed!

Hiking into the cloud on top of Quandary

7

Bierstadt - Big Enough

Date Climbed: Saturday, Sept. 8, 2007   **Elevation**: 14,060 feet
Trail Length: 7 miles RT   **Time**: 7:00am–12:30pm (5 ½ hours)

The women from my life group hiked this fourteener with me (Tori Martin, Laura Schaefer, Christine Mulloy, Peggy Manley, and Erin Reisig). We all crammed into Laura's vehicle and left Friday afternoon, but of course had to stop in Denver for a little shopping and dinner at Cinzetti's. We arrived in Georgetown at nine, and got settled in our rooms at the Super 8 (which beats car camping any day)! We were *up and at 'em* early the next day and on the trail by seven o'clock. It was very chilly, and I couldn't wait for the sun to peek over the mountain. When it did, the warmth was immediate. Bierstadt is considered one of the easiest fourteeners. It didn't look too intimidating, but its final pitch was still very steep with a lot of rock hopping. We read a few Psalms on the summit.

I look up to the mountains. Does my help come from there?
My help comes from the Lord, who made heaven and earth.
(Psalm 121:1-2, NLT)

The LORD merely spoke, and the heavens were created.
He breathed the word, and all the stars were born.
He assigned the sea its boundaries and locked the oceans in vast reservoirs.
Let the whole world fear the LORD, and let everyone stand in awe of him.
For when he spoke, the world began! It appeared at his command.
(Psalm 33:6-9, NLT)

As we sat in awe looking at the massive mountains our God created, we talked about how incredibly big and powerful He is. We agreed that if He is big enough to speak these mountains into existence, He is big enough to help us with any need and in any circumstance. It was fun to share Bierstadt with my friends, and they all seemed to enjoy it - except for Erin, who said, "Never again!"

Hiking up Bierstadt: Christina, Me, Laura, Tori, Peggy, and Erin

SUMMER 2: 2008

8

Sherman - Higher Ways

Date: Wednesday, June 18, 2008   **Elevation**: 14,036 feet
Trail Length: 5.25 miles RT   **Time**: 7:30am–12:00pm(4 ½ hours)

After falling in love with the fourteeners my first summer of hiking, I was anxious for June to roll around, so I could get back to the high country again. My husband, Scott, agreed to hike Sherman with me, which was a little surprising after a not-so-successful fourteener experience with me the previous fall.

It was a beautiful crisp morning with very little wind as we began hiking up the rugged old mining road. We were sucking air, and had to take breaks quite often. Scott kept saying, "And you love this why?" It clearly wasn't his cup of tea! My husband is a cowboy and his motto has always been: "Why hike when you can ride a horse?" But he loves me, so he wanted to join me in this new passion of mine!

When we arrived at the Dauntless Mine (12,800 feet), however, he decided that was far enough for him, and he chose to hang out with the marmots and explore the mine while I summited. When I topped the ridge, the wind was incredibly strong, but the view was spectacular. I could see mountain ranges in all directions. As I continued hiking up the narrow ridgeline with steep drop-offs on both sides, I kept stopping to wave at Scott (who was becoming smaller and smaller with the distance). When I reached the summit and looked down at him, he looked like a tiny ant. As I strained to see him, the Lord revealed to me again how incredibly *big* He is and how incredibly *small* Diane is. Oh, how I need reminded of that often!

For just as the heavens are higher than the earth, so My ways are higher than your ways
and My thoughts higher than your thoughts.
(Isaiah 55:9, NLT)

Yes, it seems like God has to remind me often that this life is not about living for me, but about living for *Him*. He alone is God, and I am not! When things don't go the way I think they should in my life, I try to remember that God sees the bigger picture. His way may be different from mine, but His way is always the best way.

I thank You Lord for revealing Yourself to me once again. Increase my faith and my dependence on You. Help me live a life of surrender to Your higher way.

Scott is happy to hang out at the Dauntless Mine

On the summit trying to see Scott at the Dauntless Mine

9 - 10
Belford and Oxford - Body Weight

Date: Thursday, July 3, 2008   **Elevation**: 14,197 feet /14,153 feet
Trail Length: 11 miles RT   **Time**: 5:30am–1:00pm (7 ½ hours)

This was the longest and hardest hike thus far! Shane hiked with me again, as a birthday present. We were up early and hiking by five thirty. It was a beautiful day but still chilly in the early morning. Shane charged right up the hill, pushing me to keep up (which is not fair because he doesn't even train). Pictures of these mountain trails are deceiving. They make the trails look somewhat easy, when in reality they are very steep and difficult.

This hike had a brutal elevation gain of forty-five hundred feet, but it wasn't over when we summited Belford. We still had Oxford to bag. Summiting Oxford required a descent off Belford of six hundred and fifty feet, before hiking up the steep slope to Oxford… and let me say, once you start hiking down, your body really screams at you when you begin hiking up again! After thirty minutes on Oxford's summit, it was back down and up Belford again before our final descent. Whew! It was definitely a leg burner!

I thought a lot about my body weight on this hike. (The Lord and I have had many discussions about my body weight throughout the years.) Like most women, I've struggled with body image issues; even to the point where I allowed bulimia to become a powerful stronghold in my life during my college years. On this hike, the Lord reminded me again of how His perfect love set me free from the body image prison I was in. It has taken years of God telling me how much He loves me and accepts me, (Ephesians 1) and years of my husband telling me how much he loves my body, but I can now walk in freedom and find security in who I am in Christ! I am no longer bound to what this world says. What matters to me is what my Savior says, and my husband says!

I praise You because I'm fearfully and wonderfully made;
Your works are wonderful, I know that full well.
(Psalm 139:14a)

First Annual *Rocky Mountain High in July*

Quandary – Saturday, July 19, 2008

What a joy to share my new passion for fourteeners with other women! Thirty women participated in the first Annual *Rocky Mountain High in July* women's hiking retreat. The women from Mitchell Berean Church included: Tori Martin, Camielle and Kasi Takuski, Chelsea Sauer, JoAnn and Mickayla Schneider, Brenda and Carlie Sinks, Jodi Sleeger, Colleen Hoff, Deirdre Amundsen, Amy Briggs, Crys Ringle, Jen Brummell, Carolyne Ewing, Kary McCafferty, Kim Hutchinson, Robin Hoxworth, and DeLinda Lackey. We met in Breckenridge on Friday, and after supper I shared a few spiritual lessons I've learned on the mountain.

The first thing I realized on this hike was how much *longer* it takes to get going in the morning when you have thirty women trying to get ready. Yikes! Somehow we all managed to get to the trailhead and hiking by six o'clock. God gave us a beautiful blue-sky day with no wind, which allowed us to stay on the summit for a long time. It was thrilling to see each woman reach the summit! Yes, all thirty women made it! We had an awesome time of sharing later in the evening.

Two people are better off than one, for they can help each other succeed.
(Ecclesiastes 4:9, NLT)

II

Longs - Light in the Darkness

Date: Thursday, August 28, 2008   **Elevation**: 14,225 feet
Trail Length: 15 miles RT   **Time**: 3:30am–3:30pm (12 hours)

Longs Peak (near Estes Park) is rightly named. The trail is fifteen miles long. Jodi Sleeger, who got the fourteener fever on the women's hike up Quandary, hiked with me. We pulled into the trailhead parking lot late Wednesday evening, slept a few hours in my vehicle, and took to the trail in the middle of the night.

It was my first experience starting in the dark, and it didn't help matters when the first sign we shined our headlamps on said GOBLIN FOREST. We stopped and prayed for courage. As we finished, two park rangers passed by, so we hiked behind them through Goblin Forest. God is good! As we hiked in the dark, God spoke to me about light…His light.

Your Word is a lamp to my feet, and a light for my path.
(Psalm 119:105)

We live in such a dark world. Everywhere you turn, sin and darkness are present, yet God's light can penetrate any darkness. God is light, and His children are to live as children of light. I didn't think a small headlamp would give that much light to walk on the trail, but it did, and I was thankful for the light it provided. Once we got above tree line, I also drew strength from seeing people further up the trail, walking in the light (similar to the Christian hike of life).

We had hiked three hours in the dark before the sun rose over the mountain, and although the sunrise was stunning, it revealed the daunting task before us. Longs Peak was still a long way off! The trail led us into a large boulder field and through a rock called the Keyhole. The rest of the mountain had a lot of exposure and required scrambling. I loved it! Finally, the summit was ours! Six hours to summit and another six to descend. A crazy long day on Longs!

12

Yale - Summit Living

Date: Saturday, September 5, 2008   **Elevation**: 14,196 feet
Trail Length: 9 miles RT   **Time**: 6:30am—5:00pm (10 ½ hours)

This was my last fourteener of the 2008 season. Delinda Lackey, Crys Ringle, Jen Brummell and Michele Jackson hiked with me. A typical schedule for a hiking trip had become: drive over the day before, sleep a few hours, get up early, hike for several hours, and then drive home the same day. Needless to say, it's very taxing on the body - but I love it! Somehow, through it all, God always refreshes and revives my soul. I may come home physically tired, but I'm always spiritually refreshed.

I enjoyed how this trail started alongside a mountain stream with a gradual incline. The smell of pine trees and the sound of rushing water gave me an extra kick in my step. But as with every fourteener, there was a very steep incline that followed. A cold wind picked up as we gained elevation, but the skies were blue, so we labored on. We scrambled up the last section and gained our summit, but due to the cold winds we began our descent quickly.

After two summers of hiking fourteeners, I began to realize I had another misconception about these mighty mountains. I thought I would be spending a longer time on the summits. In fact, I packed my Bible and journal up the first few mountains, with the picture in my mind that on each summit, I would pull out my Bible and journal, and have this holy time with the Lord, reading and listening and writing in the sunshine and beauty. I sure had the wrong picture! I learned very quickly; one does not stay on the summit very long because the weather above fourteen thousand feet is rarely pleasant, never mind the fact that it's hard to breathe at that altitude.

I don't think we're meant to stay long on the summit in the Christian hike either. We get snippets of summit living, but the majority of our Christian hike is spent in the lower country. Someday though, I will reach my final mountain summit of heaven. The weather will be perfect, and the stay will be for *eternity!* But until that time comes, I'll keep hiking.

Side note: Call me a heathen, but I no longer pack my Bible and journal on my hikes. I wait to journal in the lower, warmer country.

SUMMER 3:
2009

13

Princeton - Storms of Life

Date: Saturday, June 6, 2009   **Elevation**: 14,197 feet
Trail Length: 11 miles RT   **Time**: 5:30am–3:30pm (10 hours)

June had finally arrived again! Training gets long and tedious during the winter months, so I was once again ready to go up to the mountain and learn His ways. I was a little nervous about hiking this early in June - especially after a failed attempt to summit Laramie Peak in Wyoming (elevation 10,274 feet) the previous weekend due to snow. But the mountains were calling, and I had to go! Crys Ringle, Jen Brummell, Kim Hutchinson and Charity May joined me for this adventure.

On the morning of the hike, the weather was absolutely beautiful, but as we gained elevation, the temperature dropped dramatically. By the time we approached the upper ridge; freezing winds were blowing so strong they almost knocked Kim down twice. It was decision time. The clouds did not look good; the last half-mile of ridgeline was steep and snow packed, and the winds continued to hammer us. Two men were hiking ahead of us, and I told Kim I was going to follow them and go for it. She headed back down to meet up with the other three in our group who were hiking behind us. As I continued up the steep ridge, it became a battle not only of the body but also of the mind. I had to keep reminding myself that I was not alone; Jesus, the very one who could quiet the storm, was with me. Just as I crested the summit, the skies seemed to clear. Nevertheless, l only spent a few minutes on the summit before heading back down. When I got off the upper ridge, there came Crys and Jen, who were also determined to summit! The clouds were moving on, so I took their packs and up they went. Once we all got below twelve thousand feet, the weather was beautiful again. I am learning the only predictable thing about weather on these mountains is that it's unpredictable!

Similar to the storms on a fourteener, storms in my Christian hike of life can also appear at a moment's notice. Life can be smooth sailing, and before I know it, I find myself in the middle of a raging storm that creates fear and anxiety and causes me to doubt the goodness and faithfulness of God. Instead of asking why, I'm trying to learn to trust Jesus, knowing He has a purpose for everything that comes into my life. Whether He chooses to calm the storm or allow it to continue, He promises to work it out for good.

And we know that God causes everything to work together for the good
of those who love God and are called according to His purpose for them.
(Romans 8:28, NLT)

On the summit of Princeton

14 - 15
Shavano and Tabeguache - Slow Down

Date: Friday, June 19, 2009	**Elevation**: 14,229 feet / 14,155 feet
Trail Length: 11 miles RT	**Time**: 5:30am–1:00pm (7 ½ hours)

For Mother's Day this year, Shane said he would hike another fourteener with me, so I decided to give myself a *two-for-one* deal! We left Thursday morning because we wanted to stop by the Royal Gorge and ride the Sky Coaster (a big swing that flies you out into the canyon and back). Shane and I love thrill rides, and this one did not disappoint!

We got up at four the next morning and were on the trail by five thirty. Once we started hiking, Shane charged right up the mountain and as usual, I had to push to keep up. I don't know how many times I said, "Slow down!" but off he'd go again! After we reached the summit of Shavano, we had to descend approximately six hundred feet before hiking up again to gain the summit of Tabeguache. Then it was back down and up Shavano again before our final descent! Agonizing, to say the least!

By that time, Shane was feeling pretty queasy. He began to feel better as we descended. His strides were so long; I practically had to jog down the mountain to keep up (all the while trying to dodge rocks and keep from skidding on loose rock and gravel). The day was beautiful. The scenery was beautiful. But we moved so fast, I wasn't truly able to enjoy it. Finally, Shane said, "Hey if we keep this pace, I can make my softball game tonight at nine thirty." I just laughed! I finally knew the motivation behind his speed. There I was feeling like my fatigued legs were going to buckle at any moment, and he was thinking about getting back and playing softball. Oh to be young again!

Looking back at our hike, it reminded me of the pace I tend to keep in my Christian hike. Go, go, go… Hurry, hurry… Busy, busy… And just like I wasn't truly able to enjoy the beauty on Shavano and Tabeguache because of the speed at which we hiked, the same principle holds true in my Christian hike. I wonder how often I have missed a message or touch from God because I have been going too hard and fast to reach my destination. I am trying to be more intentional about slowing down on a daily basis, so I can hear God's voice and see His activity more clearly in my life.

Side note: Shane made his softball game and his team won eight to four!

Shavano and Tabeguache

Shane and me on the summit of Shavano

16

Humboldt - Marmot Mayhem

Date: Thursday, June 25, 2009   **Elevation**: 14,064 feet
Trail Length: 11 miles RT   **Time**: 5:30am–2:30pm (9 hours)

I had started to hike more and more with a couple of friends (Crys Ringle, Jen Brummell, and Kim Hutchinson) who love the fourteeners as much as I do, so I decided to name us the *mountain mamas*! After my Jeep had hiked herself up the nasty four-wheel drive road to the South Colony Lake trailhead, the mountain mamas were ready to take on the challenge of Humboldt. It started raining on us two miles from the summit, but we kept hiking.

The view of the jagged Crestone peaks was absolutely stunning as we hiked above the South Colony lakes. Due to threatening weather, we decided to leave our backpacks and poles at the ridge so we could hike faster. Big mistake! As we were coming off the summit, we met a couple hiking up who explained how they had to rig our packs and poles like a teepee because the marmots were having a feast! We had seen the cute and friendly looking marmots but didn't think they would bother our stuff. When we arrived back to the ridge, we couldn't believe how destructive they were in such a short time. They chewed holes in our backpacks and ate our food. They even chewed up my pole grips. It must have been *marmot mayhem*! All of a sudden, they weren't so cute and friendly anymore. Another lesson learned on the mountain.

As I hiked down the mountain, I kept thinking about the marmots and I realized in the Christian hike, Satan operates much like the mountain marmot. He subtly hangs out in the background of my life, and I don't think he's much of a threat - but he's watching and waiting for an opportunity to devour me.

The thief comes only to steal and kill and destroy.
(John 10:10a)

Be self-controlled and alert. Your enemy the devil prowls around
like a roaring lion looking for someone to devour.
(1 Peter 5:8)

God's enemy (and therefore my enemy) is Satan. I know he is stronger than I am, but he's not stronger than my God. I need to take God's Word seriously and always be on the alert for him, but I need not fear him because of the truth found in 1 John 4:4, "The One who is in you is greater than the one who is in the world." And someday, my God is going to take Satan down forever! Hallelujah!

Don't let him fool you

Marmot Mayhem

The mountain mamas on the summit of Humboldt (Kim, Jen, Crys, me)

17

Huron - Prayer Hike

Date: Wednesday, July 1, 2009   **Elevation**: 14,003 feet
Trail Length: 5 ½ miles RT   **Time**: 7:00am–11:00am (4 hours)

This was a solo hike. It was also a prayer hike. One of my friends found out she had some major health issues, so I prayed these scriptures over her as I hiked.

Don't worry about anything; instead, pray about everything.
Tell God what you need and thank Him for all He has done.
Then you will experience God's peace,
which exceeds anything we can understand.
His peace will guard your hearts and minds as you live in Christ Jesus.
(Philippians 4:6-7, NLT)

Be still, and know that I am God.
(Psalm 46:10a)

Whom have I in heaven but You? I desire You more than anything on earth.
My health may fail, and my spirit may grow weak,
but God remains the strength of my heart; He is mine forever.
(Psalm 73:25-26, NLT)

It was another beautiful day in the Rockies! I was drawn to the wildflowers on this hike. I'm amazed by how they seem to grow up out of the rocks. They are beautiful pictures of hope.

With God, all things are possible.
(Matthew 19:26b)

18 - 21

Democrat, Cameron, Lincoln, Bross -
Follow the Leader

Date: Monday, July 6, 2009	**Elevation**: 14,148 feet / 14,238 feet / 14,286 feet / 14,172 feet
Trail Length: 7 miles RT	**Time**: 6:00am–10:30am (4 ½ hours)

What a blast - bagging four fourteeners in one day! Wow! These four fourteeners (Democrat, Cameron, Lincoln, Bross) are called the Decalibron, and I wanted to summit them for two reasons: 1) to say I checked off four fourteeners in one day, and 2) to determine if they would be good possibilities for the Second Annual *Rocky Mountain High in July* women's hiking retreat. After the summits, I decided they would work great for the retreat because women would have the option of hiking more than one mountain.

The weather was chilly all day, so I kept moving and didn't stay long on any of the four summits. On Democrat, I met a young man who was a state patrolman from Buena Vista. When I asked if he was going to summit Bross (which was officially closed to the public) and he said yes, I thought, "If he is a state patrolman and he is hiking it, I can hike it too!"

When I got down off of Bross, the Lord convicted me and revealed to me that when others disobey, it doesn't give me the liberty to disobey (even if they are people in authority). *I'm sorry Lord.* Later in the day, God's Word challenged me on the importance of being a spiritual leader who leads by godly example... because, just like I followed the state patrolman, others would be following me.

In everything set them an example by doing what is good.
(Titus 2:7a)

Second Annual *Rocky Mountain High in July*

Decalibron – Saturday, July 18, 2009

The first summer I started hiking fourteeners, I didn't have any hiking friends, so I begged my family to go with me…but then I ran out of family! (Once was enough for most them.) Then I took my dog, Duke, but he didn't care for it either. The previous summer I had led a women's hike and called it *Rocky Mountain High in July*. I opened it up to any women who wanted to try a fourteener and thirty women went. It was an awesome time, and now I have several women who have the fourteener fever with me!

The Second Annual *Rocky Mountain High in July* women's hike was another successful trip. By that I mean we all made it home safely. No one fell off the mountain or collapsed with a heart attack! This year's group included: Courtney Lee, Jen Brummell, Crys Ringle, Colleen Hoff, Jana Richard, Tanya Holbrook, Marcia and Emily Bauer, Steph and Shannon Vakoc, Ruth Buck, Rachel Thompson, Amy Holzworth, Julie Lewis, Kim Hutchinson, Anita Maendl, Kay Grote, Pat Correll, Kim and Brittany Schmidt, Kenda Knudsen, Lauren Mischke, Janis and Courtney Imel, Natalie Gifford, and Kristen Siever (twenty-seven of us).

We cleaned up pretty nice after the hike.

22 - 23

Antero and Culebra - Call Me Crazy

Date: July 24-25, 2009	**Elevation**: 14,269 feet / 14,047 feet
Trail Length: 7 miles RT /	**Time**: 6:30am—11:00am (4 ½ hours)
6 miles RT	7:30am—11:30am (4 hours)

This was another solo hiking weekend. Earlier in the summer, I reserved a spot to hike Culebra (the hundred-dollar mountain) for July 25. Since it was such a long drive, I decided to hike two peaks: Antero and Culebra! I drove over on Thursday and spent the night in an old, smelly, but cheap hotel in Buena Vista. I was up early and out the door before daylight.

The trail up Antero was basically a four-wheel drive road, with lots of switchbacks. Actually, the steep four-wheel drive road to the trailhead proved to be more exciting than the hike itself. I was off the mountain by noon, so I drove to Ft. Garland where I got a room at another old, but better smelling hotel, and prepared for Culebra the next day. Culebra is on private land, and the owners charge one hundred dollars per person to hike their mountain. To protect the land from overuse, they only allow a few hikers on the mountain each weekend through the summer months (which is why I had to make the reservation). There was no trail. I just navigated my own way to the summit. I was back to the jeep by eleven thirty and home by bedtime!

I know some people think I'm crazy to go off on these hikes by myself; driving six to eight hours to get to the trailheads, then driving up very steep and rocky four-wheel drive roads in the dark, and hiking alone at times in the vast wilderness and at high altitudes. Yes, it's a little on the crazy side, but at the same time, I have incredible peace and assurance knowing my God is with me. Rarely have I felt afraid, and I like to think my heavenly Father enjoys watching me hike these massive mountains He made, as much as I enjoy hiking them.

For God watches how people live; He sees everything they do.
(Job 34:21, NLT)

24

La Plata - MapQuest

Date: Wednesday, August 5, 2009	**Elevation**: 14,336 feet
Trail Length: 9 ½ miles RT	**Time**: 5:00am—2:30pm (9 ½ hours)

What a long, but glorious day hiking La Plata Peak near Leadville! Crys Ringle, Jen Brummell, and Anita Maendl (a new mountain mama recruit) hiked with me.

I thought a lot about the importance of my map during this hike. The trailhead (as with most) started at ten thousand feet - way below tree line. That meant we hiked a few hours through the trees without being able to see the summit. People often ask, "How do you keep from getting lost on those big mountains? How do you know how to get to the summit?" My answer is, "I follow my map." From the 14ers.com website, I print a map of each trail I hike. Each map gives specific directions and is clearly defined. I study the map beforehand, and I take it with me and follow where it says to go. The maps have always led me to the summit.

In the Christian hike, I also have a map (so to speak) that gives specific directions and clearly defines which way I should go. It's the Bible! I need to study it and follow what it says because it tells me how to stay on God's trail.

The Lord says, "I will guide you along the best pathway for your life.
I will advise you and watch over you."
(Psalm 32:8, NLT)

As I've hiked more fourteeners though, I've realized that sometimes I don't rely as much on my map. I don't know if it's because I've come to know what to expect, or I think I know enough I can figure it out without a map, but it's not wise on my part. Every mountain is different and without my map, it would be very easy to get off trail and possibly lost in the wilderness.

Unfortunately, I've also experienced this in my Christian hike. After hiking a few years with the Lord, I started relying less and less on my map (the Bible), and before I knew it, I *was* off trail.

God revealed to me how needy I was for His Word and how He alone knew the way. The lesson was painful but necessary to learn. Today, I am a woman who loves the Word of God, and knows I can't survive in the wilderness of this world without it!

La Plata Peak

The mountain mamas on the summit of La Plata (me, Jen, Crys, Anita)

25 - 26
Castle and Conundrum - Revivals and Rock Slides

Date: Monday, August 31, 2009	**Elevation**: 14,265 feet / 14,060 feet
Trail Length: 8 miles RT	**Time**: 6:30am–12:30pm (6 hours)

What another great solo adventure in the Rockies! It was still dark when I got to the trailhead (west of Aspen), so I waited for daybreak and people to show up. Daybreak came, but no people, so I started up the trail anyway. After a few hours of hiking, I crested a ridge and saw four guys who were obviously hiking off trail. (They probably didn't ask for directions!) When they looked up and saw I had the trail, they turned and started hiking in my direction.

As I approached the climbing section, it began to sleet. It pelted me for fifteen minutes. I contemplated whether to turn back, but then it cleared off and I had blue skies the rest of the day. Castle was the first summit I had in solitude, and I couldn't believe how it refreshed and revived my soul, even though the time spent on it was minimal. I continued on to Conundrum, which I also enjoyed in solitude, so the Lord doubled my blessing!

It was turning out to be another amazing day in the Rockies - that is until I started the descent! For some reason, I decided to go down a different way than I hiked up, and it proved to be a bad decision. I descended down a very steep couloir which became dangerously loose as I descended. Every time I took a step, several rocks moved, and I felt like the whole mountain was going to tumble. It was the first time I felt fear while hiking the fourteeners! There was no turning back at this point, so I had to continue stepping as lightly, yet as quickly as I could to get out of danger. The thing I worried about most though was the occasional rock that flew down from above. I was experiencing the very thing I read warnings about when hiking the Elks - the flying rocks! Never was I so happy to be down a mountain than when I got off of Conundrum! I'm still amazed at how quickly circumstances can change on these mighty mountains. Whether it's the landscape or weather conditions, things can change within a matter of minutes.

I've found the same holds true in my Christian hike. I call it the highs and lows of Christian hiking. One minute God may give me an incredible one-on-one revival time with Him, and the next minute I'm in the middle of a rock slide. Isaiah 45:6b-7 says, "I am the Lord and there is no other. I form the light and create darkness, I bring prosperity and create disaster; I, the Lord do all these things." I am learning that God allows all types of experiences in my life because all are needed to grow me spiritually.

Side note: I purchased a hiking helmet on the way home!

Revival on the mountain

27

Harvard - Dealing with Doubt, Part I

Date: Monday, September 7, 2009 **Elevation**: 14,420 feet
Trail Length: 13 ½ miles RT **Time**: 5:00am–2:30pm (9 ½ hours)

Anita Maendl and I bagged this peak on Labor Day - and labor it was! We followed my standard routine of leaving the day before and driving six hours to Buena Vista in time to eat and turn in early. We were on the trail by five o'clock and hiked in the dark with our headlamps for a few hours. It was a beautiful early morning, with a full moon, clear skies, and no wind. Since the trail led to both Harvard and Columbia, we decided to wait and choose which mountain we'd summit once we got to the junction - but we missed the junction, so Harvard it was! We ended up sharing the summit with five others. I sure enjoyed hiking with Anita and getting to know her better.

It never fails that at some point on every hike, doubt seems to creep in. Can I really do this? Do I really want to go on? It usually hits when I get above tree line, and I start hiking the steepest, hardest section of the trail and I can see how far I still have to hike before reaching the summit. My leg muscles begin screaming, my breathing gets labored, my pace slows dramatically, and I start to think, "I don't know if I want to keep going."

When this happens I have learned to do three things: (1) *Look back* and see how far I've already hiked. This gives me strength and changes my thinking to, "If I've hiked that far, I can keep going!" (2) *Look within* and remember to draw on the strength Christ provides. I've learned to stop, catch my breath, and ask the Lord for more strength. (3) *Look around* - not at the mountain but at those hiking on the trail beside me. On this day, I gained strength from Anita by thinking, "She is doing it, and I can do it too. We can do this together."

Doubt creeps in on my Christian hike, as well. It creeps in when the trail gets steep and difficult, and I don't feel like I can take another step. It's those times when life doesn't make sense, and it's not turning out like I thought it would that I begin to doubt that God loves me, that He is with me, and that He has a purpose for the difficult trail He has me on. It's at these times I wrestle with the same questions I wrestle with on fourteeners. Can I do this? Do I really want to go on?

Stop doubting and believe.
(John 20:27b)

We've hiked a long way but we're still not to the summit yet.
(Arrow shows our starting point.)

28 - 29
Ellingwood and Blanca -
Dealing with Doubt, Part 2

Date: Saturday, September 19, 2009 **Elevation**: 14,042 feet / 14,345 feet
Trail Length: 12 miles RT **Time**: 5:00am–6:00pm (13 hours)

Wow! These mountains are progressively getting tougher! Anita Maendl and Kim Hutchinson may never speak to me again! We were completely wiped out after thirteen hours of intense hiking. We summited Ellingwood together, and then they headed down while I tagged Blanca. I caught up to them on the way down.

During this hike, I sensed the Lord continuing to speak to me about doubt. Believe me - I fought some serious doubts on this day! He spoke to me about how I need to do the same three things in my Christian hike when doubt creeps in, as I do when I'm hiking the steep slopes of fourteeners. I need to:

(1) *Look back* and see God's faithfulness in my past and replace my doubts with God's Word of truth that says He is faithful. He has been faithful in my past, and He will be faithful to get me up every steep slope of life.

> *But then I recall all You have done O Lord.*
> *(Psalm 77:11a, NLT)*

(2) *Look within* and draw from the strength Christ provides.

> *For I can do everything through Christ, who gives me strength.*
> *(Philippians 4:13, NLT)*

(3) *Look around* and see the Christians who are hiking with me and be honest with them and say, "I'm struggling. Can you pray for me?" I need to allow God to strengthen me through my fellow hikers. At the same time, I want to remember that others are watching me hike. I want them to see an example of real faith and draw strength and encouragement from me.

Carry each other's burdens.
(Galatians 6:2a)

When we get together, I want to encourage you in your faith,
but I also want to be encouraged by yours.
(Romans 1:12, NLT)

Yes, God has created us for community. Christians need each other! I want to trust God as He gives me strength to slug up the steep slopes of life, knowing His strength comes through His Word *and* His people.

A walk through the aspens

30

Massive - An Attitude of Gratitude

Date: Saturday, October 3, 2009	**Elevation**: 14,421 feet
Trail Length: 8 miles RT	**Time**: 6:30am – 1:30pm (7 hours)

Wow! I can't believe I summited eighteen fourteeners this summer! I can't believe Scott let me summit eighteen fourteeners this summer! This brings me to the lesson God seemed to have me focus on while I was hiking Massive: *having an attitude of gratitude!* I have so much to be thankful for! I am a blessed woman to have a good and gracious God who watches over and protects me on these hikes; a good and gracious husband who allows me to go on these mountain adventures even though it's hard on him; and the good health and fitness to be able to endure these physically challenging hikes. If I never get to summit another fourteener, I want to have a thankful heart for what I have been allowed to do. Thank You Lord! Thank you Scott! I cannot adequately put into words what these mountain treks do for my soul. I only know God has used them to remind me time and time again of who He is and who I am. He has renewed and replenished me in ways I can't express.

The Sawatch Range had received a fresh dusting of snow the night before I hiked, and the snow combined with the fall colors made it one of the prettiest hikes thus far! God *wowed* me again with His creation, this time with a colorful and sparkly day to close out my 2009 hiking season!

On my way down Massive, I met several people going up and thought to myself (as I often do), *"I'm so thankful I'm not them! I'm so thankful the steep climb is over for me."* In a spiritual sense, it reminded me of an older Christian looking at younger Christians (who are just starting the "steep climb" of walking by the Spirit and not the sinful nature) and thinking, *"I'm so glad I'm over that."* Not that we ever completely conquer the battle between the Spirit and the flesh, but there seems to be a point in every believer's life, after the initial joy of salvation, that the real battle (or climb) begins as the Spirit reveals areas of your life that are not pleasing to Him, and it's sheer agony for a while as you climb the steep slope of surrender! Galatians 6:1-5 has a warning about how older believers should not look down on younger believers, but come alongside them and help them with a watchful, prayerful attitude, or they too could be tempted and fall. We *all* continually need the grace that is found in Jesus Christ our Lord.

Give thanks to the Lord, for He is good; His love endures forever.
(Psalm 107:1)

A fresh-fallen snow the night before made the mountains sparkle.

On the summit of Massive

SUMMER 4:
2010

31 - 32

Missouri and Columbia -
Selfless Hiking

Date: June 18-19, 2010	**Elevation**: 14,067 feet/14,073 feet
Trail Length: 10 ½miles/11 ½miles	**Time**: 5:30am – 4:30pm (11 hours) / 5:00am – 3:00pm (10 hours)

It was a long winter of training, but the training paid off as I decided to start the 2010 fourteener season with a double summit weekend: Missouri one day, Columbia the next! Somehow I talked the mountain mamas (Anita Maendl, Kim Hutchinson, Crys Ringle, and Jen Brummell) into joining me for this double dipper! We arrived in Buena Vista Wednesday evening, and got our packs ready for the first day's hike. Five women sharing one hotel room always makes things interesting. I slept on the rollaway mattress between the two beds. The three-thirty alarm seemed to come too fast, but we'd set it early because we knew it would take longer for five of us to get ready and on the trail (which it did)! We started hiking at five-thirty, and it was a beautiful blue-sky day. Most of the snow was melted, except for a few icy patches toward the top. It was very cold and windy on the summit, so we didn't stay long, but as we hiked below the tree line, it warmed up considerably, and we took time to stop and soak in the sunshine! Temperatures can sure vary at different altitudes on these fourteeners!

On day two it was only Crys, Jen, and me hiking Columbia! These two are a hoot! After hiking Missouri, they spent the night sitting on the hotel bed with ice packs on their knees, but by day two, they were ready to take another pounding! One word describes Colombia: *loose*. On the way down I got some great pictures of Crys and Jen doing the *butt-scootin' boogie!*

The lessons learned on these hikes were patience and selflessness. When I hike alone, I get to start on *my* time table, hike at *my* pace, stop when *my* body says, and start again when *my* body says start. But when hiking with a group, I have to consider others' needs. It got me to thinking about the Christian hike, and how we aren't made to hike alone. We are made for community, hiking alongside others.

Truthfully, sometimes I like to solo hike, but solo hiking (on mountains and in life) can lead to selfishness. Besides, the mountain mamas sure have a lot of fun sharing, laughing and learning together along the way. We also motivate each other when the hiking gets tough, keep each other from getting lost, and help each other up when we fall (similar to the body of Christ hiking together in life). For me, the benefits of group hiking far outweigh any solo hikes I've taken!

Don't be selfish... Be humble, thinking of others as better than yourselves.
(Philippians 2:3, NLT)

An icy slope on Missouri... a slip from here could have caused serious injury

33

Holy Cross - Holy Mosquito

Date: Friday, June 25, 2010   **Elevation**: 14,005 feet
Trail Length: 11 ½ miles RT   **Time**: 5:00am — 4:00pm (11 hours)

I had a little anxiety about this mountain for two reasons:

1) the thousand-foot canyon you had to hike down and up- both directions, and
2) the stories of several hikers getting lost on the downhill talus slope.

Anita Maendl hiked Holy Cross with me. It was such a beautiful morning; we were shedding layers by seven thirty. We were enjoying the rarity of hiking in T-shirts so early in the morning - that is until we reached the bottom of the canyon and were attacked by a mob of mosquitos. Thankfully Anita had one repellent towelette that we shared to keep them off while we hiked out of the canyon. The last two miles of the hike was a steep talus slope that seemed to go on forever, but we finally summited at eleven thirty. We didn't stay long though because the weather forecast called for an early afternoon thunderstorm, and we still had a few hours of hiking (including the canyon) to get to safer ground below the tree line.

On the way up we had paid careful attention to the location on the talus slope where we would need to turn on the way down, so that was not an issue. But hiking back down into the canyon and getting attacked by the mosquitoes again *was* a big issue because this time we didn't have any repellent. The mosquitoes were relentless and annoying. We were exhausted and needed to rest, but each time we stopped they would attack, so they kept us moving.

Another hour later we were back to the vehicle and the moment we got in, we heard the first clap of thunder! Anita commented that maybe God used the annoying mosquitoes to keep us moving so we wouldn't get caught in a thunderstorm.

Her comment caused me to wonder how often He might be protecting me from danger in my Christian hike (sometimes by using annoying things like a traffic light, a long train, or a lost pair of glasses), and I don't even realize it. I just get annoyed. The next time this happens, I want to stop, 'remember the mosquito' and realize that maybe; just maybe, God is protecting me from danger.

For He will command His angels concerning you
to guard you in all your ways.
(Psalm 91:11)

A moment of praise on Holy Cross

34 - 35
Challenger and Kit Carson -
The Daily Grind

Date: Monday, July 5, 2010	**Elevation**: 14,081 feet / 14,165 feet
Trail Length: 14 miles RT	**Time**: 3:30am–7:30pm (16 hours)

Wow! This was the biggest and toughest climb so far! It was definitely the longest time I've taken hiking a fourteener. Amy Holzworth bagged these two peaks with me. She caught the fourteener fever on our group hike the previous summer, so it was fun to get better acquainted while hiking with her. We started hiking in the middle of the night, and the mosquitos were thick. But after Holy Cross, I was prepared, and we had already lathered ourselves in deet! When we shined our headlamp onto the first sign, it read, "HIKE WITH CAUTION. YOU ARE IN BEAR COUNTRY." For two women hiking in the dark, it wasn't the kind of sign you like to read. We didn't have any bear deet! We made sure to keep our conversation loud and continuous, and before we knew it, daylight had come.

The next obstacle was hiking up the steep, loose gully of Challenger - and challenging it was! We summited at ten thirty under a beautiful blue-sky, but didn't stay long because it was a double-summit day. To reach Kit Carson we had to descend five hundred feet before a fun scramble up to the summit. Once we reached the top, we could see several fourteeners. It was another short stay because we knew we had a long hike down. Seven *long* hours later we saw the Jeep.

During this hike, I felt the Lord impress on me again on how very little time is spent on the summit. When you start adding up all the hours of training - the day-to-day grind through the long winter months of stepping onto the treadmill or elliptical (when it's the last thing you feel like doing) - and add that to the hours it actually takes to hike the mountain itself, the summit time is a very small fraction of the total time. The same holds true in the Christian hike. I've had many incredible spiritual summits, but I've found the majority of my

Christian hike is about the *daily grind* – the moment-by-moment choices to live for Christ and not for self; to act on His Word instead of my feelings; to obey when no one else is watching, and to live out the following verse.

> *Always be joyful. Never stop praying. Be thankful in all circumstances,*
> *for this is God's will for you who belong to Christ Jesus.*
> *(1 Thessalonians 5:16-18, NLT)*

Lord, help me be joyful, prayerful and thankful in the *daily grind* of life.

Amy and me on the summit of Kit Carson

Third Annual *Rocky Mountain High in July*

Elbert and Huron – July 17-18, 2010

Once again the Lord taught us, protected us, and brought us safely off the mountain! The 3ʳᵈ Annual *Rocky Mountain High in July* was a smaller group, so we decided to add an optional second fourteener on Sunday. This year's group consisted of fourteen women: Jen Brummell, Crys Ringle, Anita Maendl, Kim Hutchinson, Michelle Arnold, Amy Holzworth, Ruth Buck, Rachel Thompson, Pat Correll, Jana Richards, Marcia Bauer, Emily Bauer, and Mindy Fillingham. Thirteen women summited Elbert on Saturday, and nine women summited Huron on Sunday. Both days were absolutely beautiful! On Sunday, we got up at two because several women wanted to experience hiking in the dark. There were definitely some grumpy 'tudes from getting up that early, but it's pretty hard to stay grumpy when the sun comes out, and you see the views from atop a fourteener! Hiking in a larger group also works on my 'tude, because everything takes longer.

On the flip side, I have experienced great joy in seeing the faces of several women as they reach the summit each year. Faces of joy! Faces of amazement! Faces of accomplishment! Faces of worship! Like I told them during our Friday evening sharing time, what else is a PE teacher turned pastor's wife to do? I can't sing or play the piano, so I guess I'll just keep taking women on fourteener hikes!

36 - 37
Pyramid and Sneffels -
Looking Back but Pressing On

Date: August 10-11, 2010   **Elevation:** 14,018 feet / 14,150 feet
Trail Length: 8 miles RT / 4 miles RT
Time: 5:30am–3:00pm (9 ½ hours) /7:00am – 10:00am (3 hours)

I had to wait three weeks for the weather to clear so I could hike these two peaks. Pyramid is considered the third-toughest fourteener in Colorado, and I was excited for the challenge. Due to its difficulty and nasty reputation for loose rock, I knew it wouldn't be wise to hike solo (and none of my hiking friends were ready for Pyramid), so my plan was to arrive at the trailhead parking lot before dawn and pray God would bring someone along to hike with me. Faith or folly? Different people would probably give different answers, but-none-the less, I got to the trailhead parking lot at four o'clock and started praying.

The Maroon Bells trailhead shares the same parking lot, so it was disappointing to find out all the hikers in the first five cars were going up the Maroon Bells. Finally at five thirty, a young man walked by my Jeep and said he was hiking up Pyramid and didn't mind me tagging along, so off we went. Within the first hour of hiking, I found out his name was R.C., he was a college student, a firefighter in training, and a believer, so praise God for answered prayer above and beyond what I was asking! Hiking Pyramid was a blast! It was definitely steep and loose in spots, but I loved it! I especially loved climbing the green wall at the top. I came away from the mountain with the confidence I could summit all fifty-eight fourteeners!

After saying goodbye to R.C., I jumped in my Jeep and headed towards Ouray (where Sneffels was located). To get to Ouray, I had to drive through a town called Delta, where Scott and I lived the first few years after we were married. Delta was where our second child, Shane, was born. Except for Shane's birth, Delta does not hold good memories for me. It was a dark time in our marriage and in my life personally. As I drove through the town, I cried as I remembered my unfaithfulness to Scott and how my sin almost ended our marriage. It was as if the Lord was saying, "Diane, don't forget who you were before I saved you."

I was thankful for this reminder because I have a tendency to forget. I sometimes look down on people who are living in sin. I get impatient with new believers who are still so attached to the things of this world. I forget that I too have traveled that road. It was a hard valley to drive through, but afterward I rejoiced in the God of my salvation.

Restore to me the joy of your salvation.
(Psalm 51:12a)

When the Lord saved Scott and me, He completely changed our hearts toward each other. I love Scott more today than I ever thought I could. He is an amazing man, husband, father and pastor. I can't believe I get to be his wife! When I reflect on what God has done in our lives, I feel the same way King David must have felt when he said, "Who am I, O Sovereign Lord, and what is my family, that you have brought me this far?" (2 Samuel 7:18)

By the time I got to Ouray, I was completely spent – physically and emotionally. I went to bed thinking there was no way I could wake up and hike another fourteener, but "God's mercies begin afresh each morning" (Lamentations 3:23, NLT) and I got up and was on the trail again by seven o'clock. Sneffels was a solo hike, and I loved the quiet time with the Lord and the fun scramble to the top. There were other people along the trail, so I wasn't completely alone, but I enjoyed the summit in solitude.

No, dear brothers and sisters, I have not achieved it,
but I focus on this one thing: Forgetting the past
and looking forward to what lies ahead,
I press on to reach the end of the race and receive the heavenly prize
for which God, through Christ Jesus, is calling us.
(Philippians 3:13-14, NLT)

Taking a leap of faith across a narrow canyon on Pyramid

On the summit of Pyramid

38

Wetterhorn - The San Juan Marathon

Date: Monday, August 16, 2010	**Elevation**: 14,015 feet
Trail Length: 7 ½ miles RT	**Time**: 5:30am—11:00am (5 ½ hours)

I decided this would be the year to start bagging a few San Juan fourteeners. Since the San Juan Range is in the southwest corner of Colorado and it takes a day's drive just to get there, I decided to take a week of vacation and hike as many as possible in one week. I called it my San Juan Marathon vacation! I invited one of my hiking friends, Anita Maendl, to go with me, and she was very excited until she heard my goal: six fourteeners in five days! She thought I was nuts, but she still accepted my invite. It was a long eight hour drive to Lake City, where I'd made reservations at a place that boasted of cozy little cabins at a cheap price. They were cheap all right — old, musty furniture, a tiny bathroom with a rusted-out shower, and a small kitchenette with extension cords hanging on the walls and wrapped around into the living room area because there was only one outlet in the entire space. It was a hoot! We kept saying all week, "It beats living in a tent!"

Not that I was ever in need,
for I have learned to be content with whatever I have.
(Philippians 4:11, NLT)

On day one of the San Juan Marathon we hiked Wetterhorn. It became one of my favorite fourteeners. It wasn't extremely long. It had a nice, soft, grassy path through the boulder section and lots of fun scrambling at the top. I would love to hike it again. The clouds started building before noon, so I was glad we'd started early and were back down before the thunderstorms came. The best part was we didn't have to drive all the way back to Nebraska. We had a cozy cabin waiting for us, and we were able to read and relax for the afternoon. It was a great start to the San Juan Marathon!

The San Juan mountain range is spectacular

39 - 40

Redcloud and Sunshine -
Rocks in my Life

Date: Tuesday, August 17, 2010   **Elevation**: 14,034 feet/ 14,001 feet
Trail Length: 10 miles RT   **Time**: 5:30am–2:00pm (8 ½ hours)

On day two of the San Juan Marathon, we hiked Redcloud and Sunshine. I couldn't believe I'd hiked forty fourteeners. How exciting! This trail made one big loop, so we hiked down a different way than we hiked up. The route down took us through some nasty loose rock and Anita ripped her pants doing the *butt-scootin' boogie*. It was pretty funny!

As I hiked up Redcloud, I started thinking about rocks. From a distance, each mountain looks like one big rock, but as you hike to the top, you see they are made of huge piles of rocks. It made me think of the church. (By church, I mean the group of people, not the building). People outside the church looking in should see one solid unit, but as they get closer, they should see how the church is made up of many people with different colors, shapes, and personalities.

I thought about the piles of rocks (cairns) on the trails and how they help you stay on the right path, just like the church helps you stay on the right path. Then I thought about the individual rocks (people) in my life. I started to think about and pray for each staff member at Mitchell Berean Church, where I serve. I thanked God for how each one of them had been a rock in my life. As I prayed for them, I decided to find rocks that symbolized who they are, and their role in our church. When I got back from my trip, I presented them with their rocks at the following week's staff meeting and explained why I chose the rock I gave each person.

Later in the day, when I got back to the cozy cabin, I spent time in God's Word finding verses that speak of Jesus, my Rock and my Redeemer.

The Lord is my Rock, my fortress and my deliverer.
My God is my Rock in whom I take refuge.
(2 Samuel 22:2-3a)

Trust in the Lord forever, for the Lord, the Lord, is the Rock eternal.
(Isaiah 26:4)

The trail leading from Redcloud to Sunshine

41

Handies - Shortcuts

Date: Wednesday, August 18, 2010   **Elevation**: 14,048 feet
Trail Length: 5 ½ miles RT   **Time**: 7:00am–10:30am (3 ½ hours)

On day three of the San Juan Marathon, I hiked Handies. Anita opted to stay at the cabin, so I hiked it solo. Three summers previously, Scott and I had attempted to summit Handies but were unsuccessful. It was a valuable learning experience for me, so I decided to include the lessons learned from my first attempt.

Journal Entry from Thursday, September 27, 2007

I continue to learn something every time I'm in these rugged mountains! My husband, Scott, and I attempted to summit Handies Peak, but three major mistakes were made, so we were unsuccessful.

Handies Peak is in the San Juan Range in southwestern Colorado. Since Scott and I were in the area for a week, Scott told me he would hike a fourteener with me. Was I ever excited! On the morning of our hike, the weather was perfect. I figured it would take us ninety minutes to get to the trailhead (seventy miles) so we didn't leave the cabin until nine o'clock. What I didn't realize was the last fifteen miles was a dirt road that got steeper and more rugged as we went. The dirt road took us ninety minutes by itself, so it was noon when we started to hike (mistake one).

By the time we started up the trail, we were both irritated. Scott was irritated because we had just traveled fifteen miles on a very rough road in our Buick Rendezvous and had scraped the bottom of our vehicle several times. I was irritated because the day wasn't turning out like I had envisioned. In our mutual irritation, we started hiking in silence. When we stopped to catch our breath, Scott said, "I must really love you if I'm doing this." which made me laugh.

As we rested, Scott looked across the large basin and saw where it looked like the trail continued up higher and said, "You know, if we cut across this basin, we would save a lot of time and energy."

I had accidentally left my trail map in the car and couldn't refer to it (mistake two), so I agreed to go off trail and cut across the basin (mistake three).

Unfortunately, when we got across the basin (which took a lot longer than we thought it would) and on the higher trail, it was *not* the hiking trail! It was a mountain goat trail! Now we were so far off trail we didn't have time to summit.

Later, as I thought about our hike, I realized the same holds true in the Christian hike. We live in a day and age where we want quick fixes and short-cuts in life. We even try to take short cuts in our relationship with the Lord. We want to be close to the Lord, but we don't want take the time or make the effort to get there.

> *This is what the* LORD *says: "Stop at the crossroads and look around.*
> *Ask for the old, godly way, and walk in it.*
> *Travel its path, and you will find rest for your souls.*
> *But you reply, 'No, that's not the road we want!'*
> *(Jeremiah 6:16, NLT)*

The "old, godly way" Jeremiah speaks of hasn't changed over the years. Our relationship with Christ only grows through spending time in the Word and prayer and spending time with other believers. I've gotten off trail many times in my Christian hike with the attitude of "No, that's not the road I want. I can find a quicker way!" only to later find out my way led me further away from God. But in His grace, the Lord has always been faithful to place me back on His trail and remind me His way is the only way!

I learned a valuable lesson hiking with Scott that day, and no, it wasn't, "I'm never taking Scott with me again!" It was, "I'm never getting off trail again!"

Side note: Three summers later (August 18, 2010), when I had the chance to summit Handies again, I was successful because I started early, I took my map, and I stayed on the trail!

The basin Scott and I crossed thinking it was a short-cut up the mountain.

42

San Luis - Angels Working Overtime

Date: Thursday, August 19, 2010 **Elevation**: 14,014 feet
Trail Length: 11 miles RT **Time**: 6:00am–1:00pm (7 hours)

On day four of the San Juan Marathon, we summited San Luis Peak. On this particular day, I was reminded that sometimes the greatest adventure of hiking fourteeners is trying to find the trailhead in the dark! Anita and I left the cozy cabin at three thirty in the morning. We estimated it would take ninety minutes to get to the West Willow Creek trailhead; instead it took over three hours. The directions were so unclear (It couldn't have been us!), and we ended up taking a wrong turn, which led us up a very steep and narrow, four-wheel drive road. We knew we were on the wrong road, but we had to keep going until we had enough space to turn the Jeep around. We had no business being on this road in the dark, but Anita was a good and gutsy driver, and my Jeep came through for us. (My job was praying out loud for God's protection; He came through for us too!) Long adventure short…we finally got the Jeep turned around and found the trailhead. We hadn't even started hiking yet, but we'd already had quite the adventure!

It was six o'clock by the time we started hiking, and the weather forecast called for scattered thunderstorms in the morning. This made me nervous because the majority of the trail was above tree line. The trail was nice and gradual for the first four miles, but the last mile of incline was a killer! By the time we hit the ridge line, the wind had picked up, and it was a hard push to the summit. A cloud was sitting on the summit and as we hiked into it, the temperature dropped dramatically. We knew we were racing against an incoming storm, but couldn't see anything, so we hustled back down after a brief time on the summit. Sure enough, the storm hit us. We made it back to the Jeep - wet, but safe!

He will order his angels to protect you wherever you go.
(Psalm 91:11, NLT)

43

Uncompahgre -
A Close Call with a Moose

Date: Friday, August 20, 2010   **Elevation**: 14,309'
Trail Length: 7 ½ miles RT   **Time**: 6:30am–11:00am (4 ½ hours)

Well I did it! I reached my goal of six fourteeners in five days! On day five of the San Juan Marathon, we summited Uncompahgre, and it was a perfect finale to the marathon. On the way up, we ran into a man who was hiking down. He asked if we had seen the moose. "What moose?" we both blurted. He said he was watching us from the ridge, and we were hiking alongside a moose for a good half mile. He even showed us pictures he had taken of us hiking by the moose. I was bummed we didn't see the moose, but then again, maybe that was a good thing.

When we got back to the cabin, we showered and said, "Let's go!" We got home at midnight, exhausted but extremely thankful for the San Juan Marathon adventures.

People often ask me, "Aren't you afraid of bears or other wild animals when you're hiking?" My answer is, "Yes, sometimes...but if I let my fears paralyze me, I wouldn't experience the incredible adventures I've had with the Lord." I know it's possible there have been other wild critters along the trails that saw me, but I didn't see (like the moose), but I try to keep my mind fixed on Christ and not the critters.

I can struggle with fears in the Christian hike as well - fears of failure, fears of rejection, fears of the unknown - but I know Jesus doesn't want me to be paralyzed by my fears. He has incredible adventures waiting for me when I walk by faith. If I let my fears paralyze me, I'm essentially letting Satan win the battle in keeping me ineffective for Christ. I'd rather go on the adventure any day... even if I'm a little fearful!

I prayed to the LORD, and he answered me. He freed me from all my fears.
(Psalm 34:4, NLT)

44

Lindsey - Angel Winds

Date: Monday, September 6, 2010	**Elevation**: 14,042 feet
Trail Length: 8 miles RT	**Time**: 5:00am –1:30pm (8 ½ hours)

My body was pretty fatigued after the San Juan Marathon, so it was three weeks before I was back in the mountains. Anita Maendl, Ruth Buck and Rachel Thompson signed up for this adventure. Lindsey is part of the Sangre de Cristo Range (in southern Colorado). It was a seven-hour drive to Walsenburg, where we stayed the night. We left the hotel at three o'clock in the morning and were on the trail by five. It was going to be a long day!

The weather forecast called for blue skies, but gusts of wind. As we hiked through the trees in the dark, the wind wasn't too bad, but when we got above tree line, the winds were cold and gusting so strong they knocked us off balance. As we climbed up the final steep gully, high gusts of wind would come up from the bottom and cause us to hunker down and wait until it blew over. It slowed our progress but eventually we gained the summit at nine thirty. It was so cold we only stayed long enough to take a few pictures. The winds seemed even stronger going down, and other hikers were turning around. Once we got below the tree line though, it warmed up again. I continue to be amazed at how the weather can vary so much at different altitudes on the mountain. We got back to the car at one thirty and were home by midnight.

Because the winds were especially strong on this hike, I did a word study on wind in my Bible when I got home. I came across Hebrews 1:7 (NLT), "He sends His angels like the winds; His servants like flames of fire." This verse intrigued me because on the drive to the trailhead, we talked about guardian angels. I had jokingly made the comment to the other women that I could just hear the Lord saying, "Angels, get going! My girls are climbing again!" When I found this verse, it made me look back on our hike and ponder the thought of the gusting winds being a strong and mighty presence of His angels protecting us. The commentary I read said the angels obey God's will with the speed of wind and the fervency of fire. It was a great thought for me to ponder after the very windy hike.

45 - 46

Maroon and North Maroon -

The Navigator

Date: Friday, September 17, 2010	**Elevation**: 14,156 feet / 14,014 feet
Trail Length: 10 miles RT	**Time**: 5:30am–5:00pm (11 ½ hours)

THE DEADLY BELLS

The beautiful Maroon Bells, and their neighbor Pyramid Peak have claimed many lives in the past few years. They're not extreme technical climbs, but they are unbelievably deceptive. The rock is rotten, loose and unstable. It kills quickly and without warning. The gullies are death traps. Expert climbers who did not know the proper routes have died on these peaks. Don't repeat their mistakes, for only rarely have these mountains given a second chance.

DO NOT ATTEMPT IF NOT QUALIFIED.

The above sign is posted at the Maroon Bells Trailhead. Am I crazy or what? A sign like this sure makes you stop and question whether the summit attempt is worth the risk involved. It didn't help matters that a young man died from a fall on North Maroon just a week prior to my climb. Although I had summited Pyramid earlier in the summer (and loved it), I was very anxious about this climb. This was my last hurrah of the 2010 hiking season, and it was big! Not only was I attempting one summit, I was going for the Bells Traverse (which increased the difficulty and risk even more).

I did not have any friends who were ready for this type of climb, so I went searching on the 14ers.com climbing connection page, and found two men who were experienced climbers that said I could join them. We decided to meet at the trailhead at five. The night before the hike, two more men joined our group, so now it was me and four men. I asked Scott what he thought. He said if I was climbing mountains this difficult, he preferred me to be with experienced climbers, so off I went. We met at the trailhead, had our formal introductions

(Tom, Mike, Luke, Jeff, and Diane), and into the dark mountain wilderness we hiked — me and four men! I know there are not many women who would probably do this, or many husbands who would let their wives do this, but I'm sure thankful my husband did because it ended up being the most rewarding and exhilarating day of my mountain journeys so far.

We climbed Maroon Peak first. Then we traversed over to North Maroon and came down its northeast slope, so we made one big circle. It was a beautiful blue-sky day, and the aspen trees were in full color and absolutely stunning! Several mountain goats hiked with us a various times throughout the day, so that was fun (except we had to be extremely attentive because they tend to knock off rocks).

By the time we made the ridgeline on Maroon Peak, the sun was out, and we could see the difficult and dangerous section of the mountain ahead of us. The hiking was done, and the climbing began. As we started to climb, it became evident to me how valuable Tom and his route-finding skills were to our group. He became our *navigator* which is extremely important on the Maroon Bells. He knew which gully to hike into and which gully to stay away from. His navigating skills freed me up from worrying about the route, and allowed me to focus on my climbing moves and hand holds. I loved the climbing! It was dangerous but thrilling at the same time! Finally we gained our first summit, Maroon Peak, and the view was absolutely spectacular. Jeff smoked a cigar. (I've seen several different displays of celebration on fourteener summits, but this was a first!) The traverse to North Maroon was the most difficult and dangerous section. Some climbers use ropes, but we were free climbing. Again, Tom's navigating skills were invaluable. I could see how climbers could get themselves in trouble very quickly by taking a wrong gully. We summited North Maroon early in the afternoon, and Jeff smoked another cigar. The weather remained beautiful all day, and we descended the northeast slope of North Maroon without trouble. *Thank You Lord!* When we got back to Maroon Lake (where the trail began), I took the time to gaze up at the Maroon Bells, in awe that I had just been on top of both mountains earlier in the day! I knew I had experienced something very few people get to experience.

The men ended up being great hiking partners. I learned from them and gained confidence as I climbed with them because of their experience and skill level. We gave each other high five's and departed saying we hoped to see each other on another fourteener down the road.

On my way home, I thought about the importance of having a solid navigator in my Christian hike. It's those times when life doesn't make sense, and my faith becomes weak, that I need a good navigator to come alongside me to help me regain my hope and confidence in the Lord so I can keep on hiking even when the trail is steep, hard and rough. My husband is my solid navigator! He is strong when I am weak. He is confident in the Lord when I lack faith. He leads me, and I feel safe and secure hiking with him.

Our other hiking companions for the day

On the summit of Maroon Peak: Tom, Me, Jeff, Mike, and Luke (with the cigar)

Standing at Maroon Lake with Maroon Peak and North Maroon in the background
(This picture was taken earlier in the summer after I summited Pyramid Peak)

SUMMER 5:
2011

47 -48

Crestone Peak and Needle -
A Change in Plans

Dates: July 22-23, 2011   **Elevation**: 14,297 feet / 14,197 feet
Trail Length: Day 1: To Camp, 4 miles - 1:00pm-5:00pm (4 hours)
          Day 2: Crestone Peak, 5 ½ miles RT - 6:00am-1:00pm (7 hours)
          Day 3: Crestone Needle, 7 miles RT - 5:00am-12:00pm (7 hours)

After ten long months, the snow had finally melted and I was able to bag two more mountains: Crestone Peak and Crestone Needle. I had attempted four fourteeners in the Chicago Basin (San Juan Range) earlier in the summer but failed because I was not adequately prepared for an overnight camping experience. It was a huge disappointment because my plan was to finish the rest of the San Juan fourteeners while I was on that trip, and I came home without even one. Up to this point, most of my hiking trips had gone as planned, but this one did not. I realized (in the middle of my ugly pouting session) what a bad attitude I had because my plan didn't work out. My attitude was selfish and dishonoring to God. *I'm sorry Lord.* I started thanking Him for the life and breath and health and adventures He had given me for the past five summers.

"For I know the plans I have for you", declares the Lord,
"plans to prosper you and not to harm you, plans to give you a hope and a future."
(Jeremiah 29:11)

As the heavens are higher than the earth, so are My ways higher than your ways
and My thoughts higher than your thoughts.
(Isaiah 55:9)

It reminded me of the *big* plans that had changed in my Christian hike. This past winter, God called Scott and me to leave Mitchell Berean Church (MBC) where we had ministered for nineteen years, to plant a church in Torrington, Wyoming. This was not in our plans. We loved MBC! We loved our home! We loved the community! Our plan was to stay at MBC the rest of our lives - but that was not God's plan. I would be lying if I said it was an easy process to surrender my will to God's will. It wasn't. It was one of the hardest things I've done.

But once Scott and I surrendered, the Lord gave us the peace and strength to obey. He also provided in so many ways that confirmed His call on our lives. There were definite obstacles along the way, but God was faithful to help us through each one, and in April, we said goodbye to our MBC family and moved to Torrington, Wyoming to help plant SONrise Church.

But back to the Crestones...Jen Brummell, Crys Ringle, and Megan Parker were my hiking buddies on this adventure, and we had a blast! It was Megan's first fourteener, and we initiated her well with an overnight camping experience and two difficult mountains that required both hiking and climbing.

We headed up the trail with our thirty-five-pound backpacks on a very warm afternoon and after several breaks, made it to the beautiful South Colony Lake where we set up camp. Megan was my tent buddy, and we were quite snug in my two-person tent. I didn't sleep well, but she slept like a baby.

We were up by four and on the trail by six. Our goal was to summit Crestone Peak first and then Crestone Needle, but that was before we got to the red gully of Crestone Peak and saw how long and steep it was. The gully did not surprise me because I'd climbed similar gullies on other mountains, but it caused concern for Jen and Crys. Approximately half-way up, they decided it was far enough for them and turned back down. Megan, on the other hand, was a mountain goat and scrambled right up with me. This was a big, steep mountain with a lot of loose rock at the top, but Megan seemed to love it. The fourteener fever was spreading!

By the time we got back down, the afternoon storm clouds were forming, so we opted to wait and hit Crestone Needle the next day. After a few games of cribbage and supper, it was early to bed. Jen and Crys decided to sleep in, pack up camp, and head back down the mountain, while Megan and I headed back up to bag Crestone Needle. We were very stiff and slow moving at first, but then we found our groove and made the summit at seven thirty. The rock on Crestone Needle was smooth and solid and very fun to scramble up. Coming down we got off trail twice, but still made good time and got back to the vehicle by noon.

I thought I'd sleep all the way home, but we ended up talking instead. I had prepared a short Bible study for the weekend, on keeping Christ first in our lives (from the book of Haggai), so we finished talking about the study, and that led to sharing our stories and challenges in life. I sure love these women!

Megan (our new recruit), me, Crys and Jen ready to head up the trail

Megan and me on top of Crestone Needle

49

Snowmass - Death on the Mountain

Date: Tuesday, August 9, 2011   **Elevation**: 14,092 feet
Trail Length: 9 miles RT   **Time**: 6:30am — 2:30pm (8 hours)

Megan Parker hiked Snowmass with me. She has become a great friend and hiking buddy this summer! I was impressed she was willing to go with me because Snowmass is another mountain with a nasty reputation for steepness and loose rock. As we climbed, we found out that even the larger rocks were unstable. Our summit stay was short, and coming down it felt as if the whole mountain could tumble at any moment. Maybe it was because a week prior to our hike, a young man died on Snowmass from a rock slide. I am always shaken when I hear of a death on the mountain, and I am especially shaken when it happens a week prior to my scheduled climb on the *very* mountain I'm planning to climb. These deaths always cause me to stop and remember two things:

1) There is a great risk involved in hiking these massive mountains. Some deaths have been experienced climbers who have been hiking for years. Sometimes the deaths are due to climbing error, but sometimes they are due to acts of nature. No matter the cause, these deaths remind me of the importance of staying 'in the moment' and using sound judgment when climbing. On the other hand, there is risk involved in everyday life (like driving a car), so I have peace while hiking these mountains (risks and all), because ultimately I know my life is in God's hands.

2) All people will reach their final summit someday, and no one knows when that day is - except God. I want to keep growing in Christ and learning how to make each day count for Him - so when my final summit arrives, I won't need to shrink back from my Maker but will freely and joyfully be able to worship Him for all eternity! Hallelujah!

You saw me before I was born. Every day of my life was recorded in your book.
Every moment was laid out before a single day had passed.
(Psalm 139:16, NLT)

SUMMER 6:
2012

50

Little Bear - The Transformer

Date: Friday, June 15, 2012   **Elevation**: 14,037 feet
Trail Length: 12 miles RT   **Time**: 2:00am – 1:00pm (11 hours)

The 2012 hiking season had finally arrived! Ten months is a long time between fourteeners! I was ready to put the results of *the Transformer* to the test. Since I knew my remaining nine fourteeners were among the longest and most difficult, I bought a treadmill over the winter (named it the Transformer) and stepped up my training. At first I enjoyed the Transformer because it was something new - but it didn't take long before the newness wore off, and I was bored. I questioned if it would even make a difference. There were many days through the winter months when I didn't feel like stepping on the Transformer, but I chose to anyway and over time, I began to notice changes taking place in my body. First, I started losing a few pounds. (What girl doesn't like that?) Then I started seeing definition in my muscle tone. The Transformer *was* doing its job. I was feeling stronger every day.

In the Christian hike, the Bible is the Transformer. Just like there are days when I don't feel like exercising, there are days when I don't feel like reading my Bible. I choose to anyway, because I know my spiritual training is even more important than my physical training. Over the years, God's Word has transformed my thinking and actions to help me live in a way that honors Christ.

Don't copy the behavior and customs of this world,
but let God transform you into a new person by changing the way you think.
(Romans 12:2a, NLT)

Physical training is good, but training for godliness is much better,
promising benefits in this life and in the life to come.
(1 Timothy 4:8, NLT)

Little Bear (the second-toughest fourteener in the state), would be a good test for the Transformer, and it was next on my list. Since the snowpack was less this year, I was able to schedule the hike for June. Fortunately, I was able to hike again with Tom, the navigator from my Maroon Bells group.

We met at the trailhead in the middle of the night and started hiking up *crazy* Como Road (an ankle-turning, knee-pounding, steep four-wheel drive road). By mid-morning, we had reached the hourglass gully. Our hiking was done, and now it was time to climb! The hourglass gully is considered the most dangerous gully on all the fourteeners because loose rocks often roll down the steep, narrow gully leaving climbers no space to move out of the way. Thankfully, we climbed up without any falling rocks. The summit was ours, and it was awesome to be above fourteen thousand feet again!

Since it was such a beautiful blue-sky day, Tom decided to traverse to Blanca, but I decided to head back down. That meant, however, that I had to down climb the hourglass gully by myself. It also meant I had to hike on the backside of Little Bear a couple of hours with no other hikers in sight. Yes, it involved risk, but I knew the Lord was with me, and I talked to Him all the way down the mountain. I made it back to the Jeep by early afternoon.

I was completely exhausted, but thanks to the hours previously spent training on the Transformer; I had the leg strength and stamina to endure the steep and dangerous twelve mile hike. The same holds true in my Christian hike. God's Word transforms me and develops my muscles of faith, so I can hike the steep slopes of life He leads me on. Whether it's the treadmill or the Bible, the Transformer always does its job when I do mine.

Halfway up the hourglass gully

51 - 54
Sunlight, Windom, Eolus, North Eolus - Second Chances

Date: August 8-12, 2012   **Elevation**: 14,059 feet / 14,082 feet / 14,083 feet / 14,039 feet

Trail Length: Day 1: To Camp, 6 miles - 12:00pm-3:30pm (3 ½ hours)
Day 2: Sunlight / Windom, 8 miles RT - 7:00am-3:00pm (8 hours)
Day 3: Eolus / North Eolus, 14 miles - 5:00am-2:30pm (9 ½ hours)

I'm so thankful for the second chances I've had in my lifetime, including the second chance to bag these four fourteeners. I failed my first attempt because I was not adequately prepared for an overnight camping experience. (I nearly froze!) The trailhead for these mountains is Needleton, which can only be accessed by the Silverton Train. After a three-hour ride, the train drops you off in the middle of the wilderness between Durango and Silverton, and that's the trailhead. The train ticket costs one hundred dollars, and I didn't want to pay it a third time, so I was highly motivated to get all four summits. Byron and Amy Holzworth, Randy and Anita Schanaman, and Megan Parker were my hiking buddies.

As we watched the train disappear, we heaved our thirty-five-pound packs on and started up the six mile trail to our base camp. It was a warm day, so we were thankful for the cloudy overcast. It took us three and a half hours to get to the Chicago Basin where we set up camp. After a supper of freeze-dried chicken and rice and freeze-dried ice cream sandwiches (yummy!), we called it a day.

On day two, our goal was to summit Sunlight and Windom. I tried to keep us at a good pace, knowing the thunderstorms would be rolling in the early afternoon. We summited Sunlight by mid-morning. The summit block on Sunlight requires the single-most-difficult-move on any fourteener. (It's hard to explain but trust me—it can make you pee your pants!)

As we started to climb up Windom, the storm clouds rolled in, so I kicked it into high gear and the others followed suit! By the time I summited at twelve thirty, a nasty lightning storm was taking place one mountain range away and quickly moving our direction. One quick picture and back down the mountain I headed.

Randy and Megan were close behind, and Amy was about ten minutes later, so Megan and I continued down while Randy waited for Amy. We all tried to hike down as quickly and safely as possible. Thankfully, it didn't start raining on us until we got off the steepest section. By the time we arrived back at camp, the skies had opened up, and it was a beautiful evening.

Day three was the biggest day of all. Our goal was to bag two summits and then hike all the way back down to catch the train by four o'clock. If we missed the train, we would have to spend the night at the river and wait for the train the following day, so we hoofed it again. It was only Amy, Megan and me, so we kept a pretty steady pace - that is, until we got to the catwalk on Eolus.

The catwalk was a narrow section of ridgeline with good exposure on both sides. By the looks on Amy's and Megan's faces, I didn't know if they were going to attempt it, but they took it nice and slow and ended up doing great. The slope then turned very steep and required a few difficult moves as we scrambled up the last section of the mountain. We found a better route coming down, so it wasn't as bad. We were running short of time, so they told me to summit North Eolus by myself and catch them on the way down. We made it back to the train with an hour to spare, thanks to the help of Byron, Randy, and Anita, who packed up camp. *Thank you Lord, for second chances!*

Getting ready to board the Silverton train that took us to the trailhead

SUMMER 7:
2013

55 - 56
Wilson and El Diente - His Voice

Date: July 30-31, 2013   **Elevation**: 14,246 feet/ 14,159 feet
Trail Length: Day 1: To Camp, 3 miles - 3:00pm-5:00pm (2 hours)
Day 2: Wilson / El Diente, 12 miles - 5:00am-6:00pm (13 hours)

It was another *long* winter! Training for the fourteeners during the winter months had become increasingly more difficult with age. (I turned 50 this year!) With only four fourteeners to go, I was determined to finish this summer. Amy Holzworth and I had started planning this trip several months in advance, and we had each day planned out.

Day one went as planned. We left Torrington, Wyoming, at four in the morning and got to the trailhead near Telluride at two thirty in the afternoon. As we started hiking up the Kilpacker trail, we met a man hiking out who told us he had a run-in with a bear one mile up the trail. He said the bear was sitting on the trail and wouldn't move, even when he hollered and blew his whistle. Well that put a little fear in us as we headed up the trail. (Running into a bear was not part of our plan.) We talked loudly and sang, and thankfully didn't see the bear. Maybe our singing scared him off! We found a great campsite and turned in early.

Day two also went as planned. We were on the trail by five o'clock. Once daylight hit, we were able to see the daunting task before us: miles of talus. Hiking on this particular talus was taxing on our feet and legs because the rocks were different sizes, and many of them unstable. After hiking on what seemed like miles and miles of talus, we scrambled up a steep, loose gully to gain the summit of Wilson at eight thirty. We had the summit to ourselves but only stayed thirty minutes because we knew we still had another big mountain to cover. We were sure thankful for the beautiful day!

Instead of the ridge traverse, we opted to down climb one thousand feet and then traverse. We were making our own trail and hoping we would eventually meet up with the El Diente trail, and sure enough we did. El Diente seemed even steeper and looser than Wilson, but we took our time and gained the summit at twelve thirty. Another summit to ourselves! (Not as many people hike these mountains because of the danger involved and lives lost.)

We were thankful to get off the steep slope, and by the time we got back to the car, we were both completely spent! I wonder how many rocks we stepped on during the day. Our bodies were aching, but our minds rejoicing for getting both summits. *Thank You Lord for the great weather (and no bear trouble)!*

Day three, however, did *not* go according to our plan. We were on the Rock of Ages Trail by five o'clock to tackle Wilson Peak but the weather forecast was calling for early afternoon thunderstorms. Our pace was slower because we were fatigued from the previous days hike. As we trudged along, it started to rain.

Finally at nine thirty we made it to the saddle. It was decision time. Should we keep going or turn around? We had hiked a strenuous three and a half miles, but we still had a mile to go - and the most difficult mile at that. The clouds were getting darker, and the steep section ahead was wet due to the rain. As we sat and rested a few minutes, we prayed together and asked God what to do. His voice was not audible, but it was clear…and against our own desires, we turned around and hiked back down. We rested the remainder of the day and watched the weather, hoping we would be able to summit the next morning.

Day four did *not* go according to our plan either. We had tried to sleep, but both of us were restless. All night we prayed that God would give us a very clear sign as to whether we should attempt the summit again. When the alarm went off, we woke to thunder, lightning and heavy rain. Was this a sign, Lord? (Confession time - sometimes I listen well to the voice of God and other times I don't. This was one of those *don't* times!) We decided the storm was not a clear enough sign for us, so we got dressed and drove up to the trailhead. On our way up the steep mountain road, we crossed a couple of areas where the heavy rains had washed the road out. It was dark and hard to see, and we had no business being on this steep, muddy mountain road, but we kept going. (Did I forget to mention the entire area was in a flash flood watch?) When we got to the trailhead and saw we were the only car in the parking lot, we finally gave in. We were going home without the third summit.

On the way home, I confessed my sin of not listening to the Lord. I thanked Him for keeping us safe despite our disobedience. I asked Him to help me grow in accepting that life doesn't always have to go according to my plan, and I thanked Him for not always giving me what I want, when I want it.

God had given me another incredible adventure in His mountains and a lesson on listening to Him. As I'm growing in my Christian walk, the Lord is teaching me over and over again that it is a life long journey of surrender and selflessness. Not my will, but His be done. I am still learning to obey His voice in my life.

> *...the sheep recognize His voice and come to Him.*
> *He calls His own sheep by name and leads them out...*
> *He walks ahead of them and they follow Him because they know His voice.*
> *(John 10:3b-4, NLT)*

El Diente looms in the far background

57

Wilson Peak - Finishing Well

Date: Thursday, August 8, 2013 **Elevation**: 14,017 feet
Trail Length: 9 miles RT **Time**: 4:00am — 11:00am (7 hours)

One week after getting turned around on the saddle of Wilson Peak due to weather, I was back in the San Juans chasing it again. This time I was driving alone and meeting a couple from Albuquerque, New Mexico to hike with them. I had connected with them on the 14ers.com website. Our plan was to car camp at the trailhead the night before so we could get an early start the next day. The San Juans were still getting a lot of rain, and that was a big concern of mine. Two days before the hike, I checked the weather forecast. It looked clear, so I drove to Glenwood Springs (halfway). Before I left Glenwood Springs, I checked the weather again. It now said the entire area was under a flash flood watch again. I was in such conflict and didn't know what to do, even after I prayed. I did not want to drive ten hours and be turned around again because of weather. I called Allen and Beth (the couple I was meeting), and they were on their way. I called Scott and asked him what I should do. After we talked it through and prayed, he said he thought I should go for it, so I did!

I got to the trailhead parking lot at five o'clock and was relieved to see it wasn't raining. Allen and Beth arrived an hour later, and we chatted awhile before saying goodnight. We were on the trail by four the next morning, and I enjoyed getting acquainted with them. I learned they were both pharmacists who worked seven days on, seven days off, which provided them with opportunities for fourteener trips to Colorado! It was their third summer hiking the fourteeners, and I could tell they too had the fourteener fever. As we continued to slug up the steep trail, I noticed it hadn't rained at all. *Thank You Lord.* Finally, we made it to the saddle (where Amy and I had turned around a week prior). The mountains had thin white clouds moving around them. It was absolutely beautiful and mystical! A thick white cloud was sitting on Wilson Peak but as we started to climb, the cloud lifted, which helped us see where we were going. *Thank You Lord.* When we finally summited at eight o'clock, the cloud had moved back, so we were sitting in a cloud on Wilson Peak! Very few people get this experience. *Thank You Lord.*

For ever since the world was created,
people have seen the earth and sky. Through everything God made,
they can clearly see His invisible qualities—His eternal power and divine nature.
So they have no excuse for not knowing God.
(Romans 1:20, NLT)

On the way down, I had the opportunity to share my 'God story' with Beth. (Maybe that's why Amy and I didn't get to summit Wilson Peak last week!) As I was driving home, I began thinking how crazy it was that I only had one fourteener left! It was hard to believe I was nearing the finish line. One thing I knew for sure: I wanted to finish well. Finishing well in my Christian hike has also been on my mind this summer. My parents and Scott's parents are aging (now in their seventies and eighties), and I've seen examples from them of how I want to finish.

Only God knows when I will reach the final summit in my Christian hike, but as I hike toward it, I want to finish well. I want to stay in love with Jesus and stay in love with Scott. Loving God and loving people - is what I believe finishing well looks like, and that is how I want to finish!

"Teacher, which is the most important commandment in the law of Moses?"
Jesus replied, "'You must love the LORD your God with all your heart, all your soul, and
all your mind.' This is the first and greatest commandment.
A second is equally important: 'Love your neighbor as yourself.'
(Matthew 22:36-39, NLT)

In a cloud on the summit of Wilson Peak

58

Capitol - The Final Summit...
Worth it All

Date: Friday, September 20, 2013   **Elevation**: 14,130 feet
Trail Length: 17 miles RT   **Time**: 2:30am – 6:30pm (16 hours)

It was hard to believe I had come to the end of my fourteener journey! In the past seven years, I'd spent hundreds of hours dreaming, planning, training, driving, hiking and climbing. My Jeep and I had covered hundreds of miles and my eyes had seen parts of God's creation that very few people will ever see. Simply put - I'd been blessed!

Without a doubt, I saved the hardest peak for last. Capitol reigns supreme! Had I attempted to summit this mountain in earlier years, with its level of difficulty and exposure, I think I would have turned around, but each year I gained a little more confidence in my climbing abilities on easier mountains, and I learned from watching more experienced climbers. Isn't that also true in the Christian hike? I'm thankful the Lord didn't ask or expect me to climb a spiritual mountain the size of Capitol Peak when I was a young Christian. Instead, He gave me smaller mountains to learn on. I love how He brought older, mature believers alongside me who taught me what it looks like to hike with Him and trust Him on the steep slopes of life.

I was privileged once again to hike with Tom Driscoll, my fourteener navigator! Tom was in the group I hiked with on the Maroon Bells. I also hiked Little Bear with Tom, so I thought it was only fitting to ask him if he would navigate once more for me on my finisher, Capitol Peak. He was gracious to do so! We originally scheduled this hike for the middle of August, but the rainy season seemed to last forever and we had to wait several weeks before the weather forecasted an all-clear day. Capitol was worth the wait!

We decided to meet at the trailhead, and start at two thirty in the morning. I arrived at the trailhead parking lot at seven, and there were five other cars but no people. I organized my pack and tried to sleep but it was futile. Tom pulled into the parking lot at one thirty, and we were on the trail shortly after that.

The first part of the hike was an enjoyable trail and easy on the feet. Everything was going great - that is until I slipped on a frosty log crossing a creek and fell smack on my back, soaking both gloves and one shoe. For the next two hours, I had to pump my fingers constantly to keep them from freezing, but eventually the sun came out and warmed me up. By that time, we were rock jumping up the mile-long talus slope toward K2 (a difficult thirteen thousand foot peak you have to cross to get to Capitol). K2 is where the hiking stopped, and the climbing began!

From K2 to the summit of Capitol, there were many places where I would have fallen to my death if I slipped. It was that steep and dangerous. The infamous Knifes Edge - a 30' section of pointed ridgeline with 200' drop-offs on both sides - was one of those places. Tom went first and showed me where to place my hands and feet. At times, I had to straddle the ridge and scoot across (which was hard on the crotch). It was crazy awesome! We continued to climb and finally reached the summit at eleven thirty. It had taken us nine hours! A demanding and difficult mountain indeed! My final summit was an emotional one. I had to fight back the tears. I had worked very hard and stayed disciplined to reach this goal of summiting all fifty-eight fourteeners of Colorado. I took a moment to reflect on all the hours of training and discipline. Was it truly worth it? Absolutely! It was worth it all!

And I know without a doubt when I reach my final summit in this Christian hike of life, it too will be worth it all! When I take my last breath here on earth, I know I will take my first breath in heaven, and I will look into the sweet face of my Savior and say, Jesus, You are worth it all! I will join with the angels and living creatures and elders and sing:

> *Worthy is the Lamb who was slain*
> *to receive power and wealth and wisdom*
> *and strength and honor and glory and praise!*
> *(Revelation 5:12)*

Oh, how I anticipate that day! But for now, I will keep on hiking. My fourteener journey is over, but my Christian hike continues. I want to be a woman of God who stays on His path and finishes well.

Thank You, sweet Jesus, for this spiritual journey You have taken me on and for calling me up to the mountain. You have been faithful to teach me Your ways, and I will forever walk in Your paths.

On K2 with Capitol Peak in the background

On the summit of Capitol with my fourteener navigator, Tom Driscoll

The Knifes Edge

About the Author

Diane played volleyball for the University of Wyoming (1981-1985) and accepted Christ as her Savior during her freshman year in college through the godly influence of her teammates. However, due to personal sin choices and lack of discipleship, she experienced very little growth as a new believer. When Scott and Diane were married, they brought an incredible amount of baggage into the marriage, but the Lord was working on their hearts. In 1990, Diane rededicated her life to Jesus, and Scott was gloriously saved!

In 1992, Scott and Diane left ranching, to respond to God's call on their life into pastoral ministry at Mitchell Berean Church in Mitchell, Nebraska. After serving there nineteen years, God reassigned them to Torrington, Wyoming in 2011, to help plant SONrise Church. (www.torringtonsonrisechurch.com)

Scott and Diane have been married twenty-eight years. They have a daughter and son-in-law (Courtney and Jared), who have two children, Kendall and Lincoln. They also have a son and daughter-in-law (Shane and Abby).

Diane loves working alongside her husband. She also loves to disciple younger women in the faith. But her favorite pastime these days is playing with her sweet grandbabies. She loves the title Nana!

For additional ordering information please go to:
www.facebook.com/Up To The Mountain
or email: dianemathis85@gmail.com.

Made in the USA
Monee, IL
16 January 2024

50704212R00062